I KNOW WHAT TO DO! SOCIAL SKILLS

# HOW TO COPE WITH CRITICISM

CAITIE MCANENEY

PowerKiDS press

Published in 2025 by The Rosen Publishing Group, Inc.
2544 Clinton Street, Buffalo, NY 14224



First Edition

Editor: Caitie McAneney
Book Design: Rachel Rising

Photo Credits: Cover, p.1 True Touch Lifestyle/Shutterstock.com; pp. 4, 6, 8, 10, 12, 14, 16, 18, 19, 20 Cute art/Shutterstock.com; p. 5 Prostock-studio/Shutterstock.com; p. 7 Bidzilya/Shutterstock.com; p. 9 Guntsoophack Yuktahnon/Shutterstock.com; p. 11 VALUA VITALY/Shutterstock.com; pp. 13, 19 wavebreakmedia/Shutterstock.com; p. 15 iofoto/Shutterstock.com; p. 17 anon_tae/Shutterstock.com; p. 21 Olena Yakobchuk/Shutterstock.com.



Library of Congress Cataloging-in-Publication Data

Names: McAneney, Caitie, author.
Title: How to cope with criticism / Caitie McAneney.
Description: Buffalo, NY : PowerKids Press, [2025] | Series: I know what to do! Social skills | Includes bibliographical references and index.
Identifiers: LCCN 2024028802 (print) | LCCN 2024028803 (ebook) | ISBN 9781499450484 (library binding) | ISBN 9781499450477 (paperback) | ISBN 9781499450491 (ebook)
Subjects: LCSH: Criticism, Personal–Juvenile literature. | Interpersonal communication in children–Juvenile literature.
Classification: LCC BF637.C74 M394 2025 (print) | LCC BF637.C74 (ebook) | DDC 158.2–dc23/eng/20240628
LC record available at https://lccn.loc.gov/2024028802
LC ebook record available at https://lccn.loc.gov/2024028803

Manufactured in the United States of America

CPSIA Compliance Information: Batch #CWPK25. For Further Information contact Rosen Publishing at 1-800-237-9932.

# CONTENTS

## What's Criticism?

Think about a time when you made something or did something. Then, someone made a **negative** comment. They said they didn't like it. They said you made a mistake. Ouch! Criticism can really hurt. It can be hard to **cope**.

## Hard to Hear

Criticism is often hard to hear. You may be proud of your work at first. Maybe you make a picture. You like it. Someone else doesn't like it. You may feel they don't like *you*. It may make you sad. Maybe you're angry.

## Take a Beat

First, deal with your feelings. Take a moment. Maybe go somewhere quiet and away from others. Take a deep breath in. Then breathe out. Do this until you feel calmer. You might also talk it out with a friend, parent, or teacher.

## Think About It

Now, think of what the person said. Did it focus on the "bad"? Did it make you feel like *you* are bad? Criticism focuses on what people don't want. It isn't very helpful. Sometimes it isn't fair. Feedback focuses on what people *do* want.

## Feedback Can Help

Your teacher says, "I see you drew a star. Great job! Next time, try to make the points straighter." That is feedback, not criticism. Feedback may still hurt. However, it gives you direction. It helps you see what's good—and what can be better.

## Ask Yourself

Get curious about the **situation**. Ask yourself: was it fair or not fair? Is it **bullying**? Is this person **qualified** to give me direction? For example, you want to listen to a teacher about your math skills, not a classmate. You can **ignore** some unfair criticism.

## Using Feedback

After feedback, you can decide to **improve**. Remind yourself that it is something you did. It isn't who you are. Feedback doesn't have to make *you* feel "bad" or "wrong." You can use it. Get creative. Try something new!

## Getting Help

You might need to ask for help. You can ask the other person to **clarify** their comments. They can tell you what they meant. You can tell them how it made you feel. You can ask for help from someone else, too.

## PRACTICE MAKES PROGRESS!

To deal with criticism or feedback, you can say:

"What do you mean by that? I want to understand."

"When you said that, it hurt my feelings."

"How can I do better?"

"I hear you say what you don't like. What *do* you like about it?"

## A Growth Mindset

It's important to remember that we are all growing. We learn something new every day. You may feel like you've failed. However, it was just a stepping stone to where you're going. If you keep a growth **mindset**, then you can do anything!

# GLOSSARY

**bullying:** To treat someone in a hurtful way on purpose.

**clarify:** To make something clear.

**cope:** To handle or deal with something.

**ignore:** To refuse to notice.

**improve:** To get better at something.

**mindset:** The way someone thinks about something.

**negative:** Disagreeable.

**qualified:** Fit for a job or activity.

**situation:** What's happening in a certain time and place.

# FOR MORE INFORMATION

## BOOKS

Hubbard, Ben. *How to Deal: Developing Skills for Coping*. North Mankato, MN: Capstone Press, 2021.

McAneney, Caitie. *I Get Creative to Cope*. Buffalo, NY: PowerKids Press, 2023.

## WEBSITES

**Growth Mindset**
*ny.pbslearningmedia.org/resource/growth-mindset-video/rise-and-shine-health-and-wellness-time/*
Learn more about having a growth mindset with this helpful video.

**What to Do When You Feel Stressed**
*kidshealth.org/en/kids/5-steps.html*
Criticism can cause stress. Check out some tips for how to deal with stress.

# INDEX